Freaky Facts about Natural Disasters

TWO CAN ™

MINNETONKA, MINNESOTA

Text and illustrations copyright © 2006 by Two-Can Publishing

Two-Can Publishing
11571 K-Tel Drive
Minnetonka, MN 55343
www.two-canpublishing.com

Written by Sarah Fecher and Clare Oliver
Illustrated by Gary Bines and Gary Boller
Edited by Jill Anderson
Cover design and Mac production by Joe Fahey

Many thanks to Dr. Mark Seeley, Professor and Extension Climatologist/Meteorologist
at the University of Minnesota, and Dr. Jim Walker, Professor of Volcanology and
Igneous Petrology at Northern Illinois University, for sharing their expertise.

Photographs:
Cover: © Carsten Peter/National Geographic Image Collection/Getty Images; pp. 4-5: © 2006
JupiterImages Corporation; p. 5: © Jim Reed/Photo Researchers; pp. 6, 24, 28: © SPL/Photo
Researchers; p. 9: Digital Vision; p. 10: © Adam Woolfitt/Corbis; p. 11: © Ace Stock Limited/
Alamy; p. 13: © Farooq Naeem/AFP/Getty Images; p. 14: © Robert Sullivan/AFP/Getty Images;
p. 15: © NASA/Science Photo Library; p. 16: © Corbis; p. 17: © Tony Ranze/AFP/Getty Images;
p. 20: © Alvis Upitis/The Image Bank/Getty Images; p. 22: Keiji Iwai/Alamy; p. 23: © Natphotos/
Digital Vision; pp. 25, 27: © SPL/Photo Researchers; p. 30: U.S. Geological Survey Photo Library;
p. 31: Choo Youn-Kong/AFP/Getty Images.

Library of Congress Catalog Card Number: 2005034418

ISBN 1-58728-539-8 (HC)
ISBN 1-58728-542-8 (PB)

Printed in China

1 2 3 4 5 10 09 08 07 06

What's Inside

Nature's Wild!

There's no question about it—humans are no match for Mother Nature. We can build the most sturdy structures and design tools and equipment to help predict future events. Yet massive disasters such as Hurricane Katrina and the Indian Ocean tsunami still cause overwhelming destruction.

Wind Power

A swirling tornado is fascinating to watch. But the damage to this bicycle is proof of its enormous power.

Earth's Creeping Crust

Many natural disasters, such as tornadoes, hurricanes, and lightning strikes, are caused by the weather. Often scientists can predict these weather events and give people at least a little time to prepare. But other disasters are harder to predict. These are caused by movements just below the earth's surface.

▲ The earth's surface may seem solid. But it's actually made up of many different pieces called plates that fit together like a jigsaw puzzle.

A Big, Fiery Cauldron

The earth's hard plates float on top of a layer of rock that is softer and more liquid. Most of the time the plates float peacefully, but...

...when two plates move apart, fiery magma can bubble up between the plates and flow out onto the earth's surface. This is a volcanic eruption.

Cracking Up

When plates crash against each other, or one plate slides underneath another, the ground may shift and shudder, and buildings may crumble. An earthquake has begun!

HELP IS ON THE WAY!

Disasters Are Deadly

Natural disasters are awesome to see, but don't forget that they can kill many people. Experts try to give warnings before disasters happen. But sometimes there's no time to escape. Then teams of rescuers rush to the scene to provide food, shelter, and medical help.

Clouds of Ash . . . .

A volcano is an opening in the earth's surface where lava, ash, and hot gases escape. Some volcanoes spurt out a little lava every day. Others sleep for thousands of years, then wake with a huge explosion that rips them apart.

Return of the Ice Age

Ash from volcanic eruptions in the 1500s may be to blame for a long, cool period in the Northern Hemisphere. The cold made polar ice spread south from the Arctic. Just think—polar bears could have trekked across the frozen sea to visit new lands! Could this be because volcanic ash shaded the sun?

THE SLEEPING GIANT WAKES

Mount St. Helens volcano in Washington State lay asleep for 123 years. Then, in 1980, its sides began to bulge slowly outward.

Suddenly the volcano blew its top. Scorching ash and clouds of gas flew into the air. Nearby streams were clogged with ash, killing fish and other animal and plant life.

Snow on the sides of the volcano melted in seconds and mixed with the ash, creating monster mud flows that destroyed more than two hundred homes.

Luckily, scientists had warned people living near the volcano that the blast was about to happen. Thousands were able to flee to safety.

and Rivers of Fire

Strange but True

Some types of lava travel slower than you walk. Others speed along at up to 31 miles (50 km) per hour.

HEE HEE! What did the mother volcano say to the baby volcano? I lava you!

HA HA!

▲ A fiery river of lava oozes down the slopes of this volcano, burning up everything in its path. When the lava cools, it will blanket the land in solid, gray rock.

Cast in Stone

After a volcano erupts, things are never quite the same. The hot lava and ash cool and turn into hard rocks. Many of these rocks have weird shapes. Others hide incredible secrets.

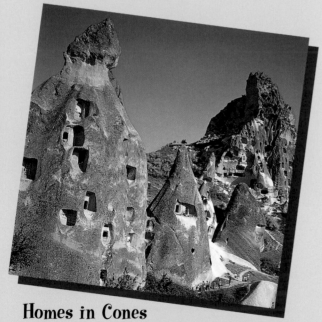

Homes in Cones

These fairy-tale cones were left by volcanoes that erupted eight million years ago in Turkey. Rain washed away the softer parts of the cones to form caves where people made their homes. Today a few people still live here.

Smothered in Ash

In A.D. 79, in Italy, a giant volcano called Mount Vesuvius erupted. It showered the town of Pompeii with scorching ash. People tried to flee. Some were suffocated by the choking gases from the volcano and dropped dead, while others were burned and buried alive.

DISCOVERING THE PEOPLE OF POMPEII

1 Centuries later, archaeologists dug into the rock at Pompeii and discovered holes in the shape of people. The bodies in the holes had rotted away a long time ago.

2 The archaeologists used the holes as molds. They poured in runny plaster of paris and waited for it to set.

3 When the plaster was dry, the archaeologists chipped away the surrounding rock. They were left with plaster models of fleeing townspeople and their pets!

Believe It or Not

Scientists have made plaster models of about 2,000 people who died in Pompeii.

▲ The plaster casts made of the bodies in Pompeii show the terrible destruction caused by Vesuvius. Some people look as if they died peacefully, while others seem to have struggled.

On the CRACK! Move

Sometimes when Earth's plates rub each other the wrong way, the ground jumps and rattles, causing an earthquake. Most earthquakes are too small for people to notice. But a major earthquake can destroy cities and even move mountains!

The Great San Francisco Fire

In 1906, an earthquake hit San Francisco, causing a double disaster. First buildings toppled over. Then broken gas pipes, electrical wires, and stoves sparked fires that burned down most of the city.

Making Waves

Earthquakes under the sea create the biggest waves in the world, called tsunamis. When a tsunami hits the coast, the massive wave may be traveling twice as fast as a racecar and may be three times taller than a house. It swallows everything in its path and then pulls it out to sea.

To the Rescue

After an earthquake, the race is on to find people trapped in the rubble. Specially trained dogs with super-sensitive noses sniff their way toward a survivor. Then they bark the good news to a rescue team, who pull the person to safety.

Believe It or Not

If one of Earth's plates moves just 8 inches (20 cm), it can set off a quake big enough to destroy a city.

▲ This apartment building in Islamabad, Pakistan, was flattened in a strong earthquake that struck Pakistan and northern India on October 8, 2005.

Wild Winds

Hurricanes are the world's fiercest storms. Their wild winds can rip up trees, blow down houses, and send seawater surging far ashore. Add some drenching rains, and you've got a recipe for disaster.

HEE HEE!

HA HA!

What did one hurricane say to the other hurricane? I've got my eye on you!

▲ On August 30, 2005, high winds and floodwaters from Hurricane Katrina made Biloxi, Mississippi, a disaster zone. Gulfport, Mississippi, and New Orleans, Louisiana, were also hit hard.

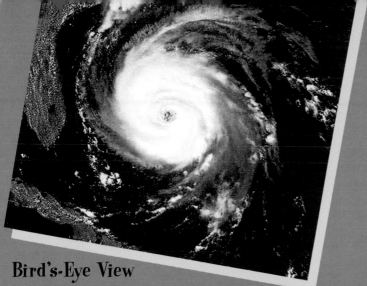

Bird's-Eye View

This photograph, taken from space, shows a hurricane spinning toward the Florida coast. The most dangerous winds and the heaviest rains lurk in the thick, white part of the storm.

Tricked You!

The center of a hurricane is called the eye. Winds in the eye are fairly calm. When the eye passes over, you may even be able to see blue sky or stars! It may seem as if the storm is over, but really you're right in the middle of it. Spooky!

What's in a Name?

Hurricanes are named to make them easy to identify. The first person to name these storms was a weather forecaster who lived in the 1800s. He named them after people he didn't like! Now, an international group of meteorologists keeps a list of men's and women's names.

PEOPLE I DON'T LIKE

P.T.O

Tell Me Why

SANDSTORMS KICK UP TROUBLE

I sure could use a shovel.

In Egypt, strong winds fly across the desert and whip up wicked sandstorms called haboobs. The winds can smother whole villages, and even the ancient pyramids, in clouds of sand and dust.

Millions of years ago, huge sandstorms raged through the Gobi Desert in Asia, burying dinosaurs and their eggs. The hot sand kept the eggs perfectly preserved. Now the Gobi Desert is a popular spot for dino experts to come to dig for fossils.

Terrible Twisters

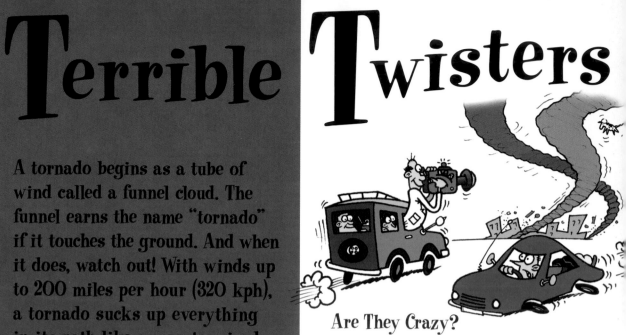

A tornado begins as a tube of wind called a funnel cloud. The funnel earns the name "tornado" if it touches the ground. And when it does, watch out! With winds up to 200 miles per hour (320 kph), a tornado sucks up everything in its path like a monster-sized vacuum cleaner.

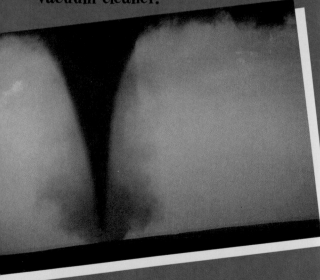

Touchdown!

When a tornado touches down, it makes a deafening roar. Many people say it sounds like a freight train is barreling toward you. Because this tornado landed in an open field, it kicked up a lot of dust but didn't cause any serious damage.

Are They Crazy?

When most people see a tornado, they take off quickly in the opposite direction. But storm chasers don't. They follow after it, in hopes of capturing great photos and video of the storm.

Lucky Escape

In 1986, in China, a tornado picked up twelve schoolchildren and carried them through the air for 12 miles (19 km). When it put them down again, they were completely unharmed!

▲ These homes in Florida were ripped apart by a powerful tornado. A twister may stay on the ground for several minutes, or it may touch down briefly and lift right back into the clouds.

Flood Alert

Rain is the all-time biggest cause of natural disasters. Short, heavy downpours flood homes and streets. Nonstop rain leads to even bigger trouble. Rivers overflow their banks, sending muddy water rushing everywhere. Hillsides turn to mush and wash away.

That's Weird

Floods even happen in deserts. When a storm breaks out in nearby hills, water races down the slopes. Then it surges along channels in the dry desert, sweeping up everything in its path.

Spring Thaw

Rain isn't the only cause of flooding. In areas that receive lots of snow, a rapid warm-up in the spring can mean big trouble. The melted snow can't soak into the ground fast enough and floods the landscape, sending people and animals scurrying for higher ground.

High and Dry

In some hot, wet countries, people live high off the ground in houses on stilts. These people know that every year during the rainy season, it will rain heavily for days on end. While more traditional homes may be soaked or even washed away, these smart people stay safe and dry in their high-rise homes.

▲ Much of New Orleans was underwater after Hurricane Katrina hit in 2005. Wind and waves broke down walls called levees, sending the waters of Lake Pontchartrain pouring into the low-lying city.

White-Out!

Blizzards are dangerous winter storms. High winds mix with snow to create dangerous white-outs that bring travel to a standstill. Winter ice storms cover the landscape in a slippery blanket that snaps trees and power lines and traps people in their homes.

Believe It or Not
Each year, the Rocky Mountains experience about 100,000 avalanches. Luckily, people are rarely hurt.

Monster Drifts

Blizzards are a deadly duo of heavy snowfall and strong winds. The bone-chilling blasts quickly drive snow into massive piles called drifts. The most monstrous drifts can be three or four times taller than an adult. That's high enough to bury a house.

Avalanche on Its Way!

Mix a snowstorm with a mountain, and you've got a recipe for an avalanche. When snow on a mountainside grows too heavy, it suddenly breaks free. As the icy load tumbles down the slope, it picks up speed—and more snow—until millions of tons of snow roar downhill, sweeping up anything, or anyone, in its path.

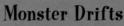

FINISH

During World War 1, avalanches were used as weapons. Soldiers fighting in the mountains of France fired guns at snowy ledges above their enemy's camps. The sound waves from the shots set off avalanches that buried the camps in snow.

Today experts fire special guns at snow above mountain villages as a way to protect people who live there. The small explosions cause harmless mini-avalanches. This keeps the snow from building up and setting off a huge, killer avalanche.

▲ A snowplow tries to keep an airport runway cleared during a blizzard in Minnesota.

Dry Spell

A drought is a period of hot, dry weather that may go on for months or even years. During a serious drought, streams and wells dry up, crops die, and soil turns to dust.

Thirsty Work

Day after day of scorching heat bakes the earth until it cracks. Cattle kick up dust as they shuffle across the bone-dry ground in search of food and water. They may trek hundreds of miles before coming across a watering hole.

A BIG BOWL OF DUST

In the 1930s, a drought hit the central United States. Many years of hot weather and little rain made it impossible to grow many crops.

With no plants to hold down the soil, winds blew the topsoil away. Blinding clouds of dust blocked out the sun and choked the birds.

Millions of people abandoned their homes. They left a string of empty ghost towns that stretched all the way from Texas to Canada.

▲ During a drought, even large trees and bushes dry out. The tiniest spark can set off a raging fire that burns for days.

Disaster

Scientists
WATCH THE SKIES

Scientists who study natural disasters are looking for trouble! They fly into storms and climb volcanoes to gather all the info they can. They can't stop disasters, but they can work to improve warning systems so that people have more time to prepare.

THE WEATHER WATCHERS
Meteorologists work in weather centers, where they gather all kinds of information about dangerous weather. They watch how weather changes and where it's heading.

Satellites high above Earth beam back pictures of clouds.

Crews on ships and in airplanes send in weather reports from faraway places.

Volcano Doctors
Volcanologists are a bit like doctors. They have the hot job of studying volcanoes. First they check a volcano's sides to see if they are bulging with hot magma. Then, the hot docs prod the volcano with a gas detector, looking for signs of escaping gases.

WEATHER CENTER

Radar picks up signs of rain, snow, wind, and tornadoes.

Inside the weather center, super-fast computers make sense of all this information.

Jeepers Creepers

It's difficult to tell when an earthquake will happen or how big it will be. A clever machine called a creepmeter helps scientists predict earthquakes. It picks up tiny shivers in the ground that could mean something much bigger is on the way.

That's Weird

Often animals give the first warning of an earthquake. Worms, snakes, rats, and mice have been known to scramble out of their holes just before the rumbles start.

▲ These scientists are launching a giant weather balloon. Its onboard equipment will measure what's happening in the clouds.

Trouble Ahead?

It's a fact—the world is getting warmer. Every day, humans pump gases into the delicate atmosphere above the earth. No one really knows what will happen next or if new kinds of natural disasters lie ahead.

Turning Up the Heat

Earth is kept cozy and warm by gases in the atmosphere that trap some of the sun's heat. Without these "greenhouse gases," the earth would be deathly cold. But pollution from cars, power plants, and factories has changed the balance of gases in the atmosphere. There is more heat-trapping carbon dioxide in the atmosphere now than ever before.

There is too much carbon dioxide reaching the atmosphere.

When factories and cars burn fuel, they release carbon dioxide.

That's Weird

When cows breathe (and burp!), they give off huge amounts of a world-warming gas called methane.

Meltdown

Some scientists fear that the world could become so warm that the ice at the North and South Poles will melt. The melting ice would begin to release huge amounts of water into the world's oceans. Low coastal areas would flood, and islands in many parts of the world would disappear underwater.

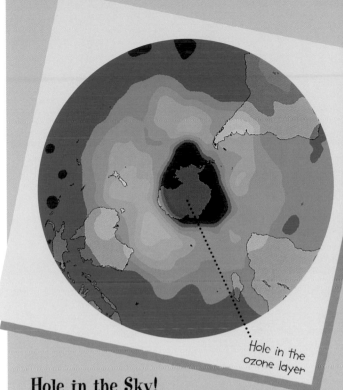

Hole in the ozone layer

Hole in the Sky!

All around the Earth, there is a layer of invisible gas called ozone. It protects our skin from the sun's harmful rays. But now scientists have spotted a hole in the ozone layer, and some of those deadly rays are getting through.

Bigger, Badder Storms?

Could a warmer world mean more severe hurricanes? Baby storm clouds feed off the steamy air that rises from warm water, so it is possible, but scientists don't all agree. They are still studying possible links between global warming and meaner hurricanes.

Frightful Fridges

Some of the villains causing the ozone hole are spray cans and refrigerators. These household objects often contain chemicals called chlorofluorocarbons, or CFCs. These nasty chemicals escape into the atmosphere and gobble up the ozone that floats there.

Hot Spots

Several places are in the hot seat when it comes to natural disasters. These hot spots are more likely to be hit than anywhere else in the world. Here's a guide to the danger zones.

Ring of Fire

North America

Europe

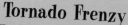

Tornado Frenzy
Each year, about 1,000 tornadoes spin across the United States. Most happen in the Midwest.

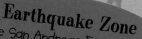

Earthquake Zone
The San Andreas Fault is a long stretch of shaky ground along the coast of California. Here, big cities are on high alert for earthquakes.

South America

Not a Drop
The Sahel is a region on the southern edge of the Sahara Desert, in Africa. For up to three years at a time, this hot, dusty area may have no rain at all.

Pacific Ocean

Ring of Fire

Key

 tornadoes

 droughts

 volcanoes

 floods

 earthquakes

 hurricanes

 icy winds

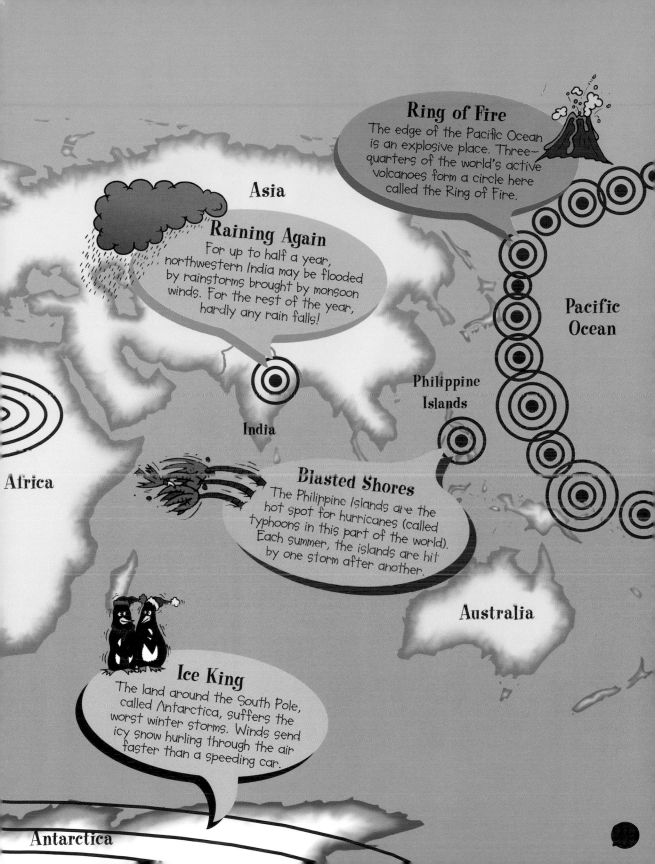

Disaster Hall of Fame

Natural disasters are the source of amazing power and tremendous tragedy. Here are some that will go down in the record books.

A Whole Lot of Shakin'

The largest earthquake to occur in the United States struck Prince William Sound, Alaska, in 1964. The huge quake caused a tsunami, landslides, and avalanches. Around the world, there are about 500,000 measurable quakes every year, but only 1/5 of these can be felt without special equipment, and only 100 of them cause damage.

Tri-State Terror

The Tri-State Tornado of 1925 goes down as the deadliest tornado in history. It stayed on the ground for 3½ hours as it tore a path through Missouri, Illinois, and Indiana. Nearly 700 people were killed.

Terrible Trio

In May 1970, the town of Yungay in Peru was hit three times in a row. First its residents were shaken out of bed by an earthquake. Next the town flooded, and finally it was engulfed by a monster mudslide.

Wall of Water

On December 26, 2004, a powerful earthquake in the Indian Ocean triggered a massive tsunami. There was little warning when the wall of water flattened coastal areas including the city of Banda Aceh, Indonesia, shown above. Over 150,000 people in southeastern Asia and eastern Africa were killed.

The Blizzard of 1888

On March 11, 1888, people on the East Coast were in for an unpleasant surprise. After several warm, sunny days, a powerful blizzard moved in. For four days, heavy snow fell. Temperatures dropped, and wind blew the snow into towering drifts. Rescue workers couldn't even get out to help people. Up to five feet of snow fell in some areas, and over 400 people died.

Tricky Words

archaeologist: a person who learns about the past by studying old buildings and ancient remains

ash: tiny, dust-like pieces of rock that are produced during some volcanic eruptions

carbon dioxide: a type of gas in the earth's atmosphere that holds heat close to the earth. Cars and factories create more carbon dioxide than the earth needs to keep warm.

lava: hot, liquid rock that may spurt out of a volcano during an eruption.

magma: hot, liquid rock lying deep under the ground

meteorologist: a scientist who studies weather

methane: one of the gases that helps to keep Earth warm

monsoon: winds that bring heavy rain at particular times of the year

ozone: a layer of gas high up in the atmosphere that protects us from the Sun's harmful rays

tsunami: a giant sea wave set in motion by an underwater earthquake or volcanic eruption

volcanologist: a scientist who studies volcanoes

Index